THE
OF
KING TUT

by Daphne Greaves

SCHOOL PUBLISHERS

Printed in China

ISBN 10: 0-15-350537-0
ISBN 13: 978-0-15-350537-9

Ordering Options
ISBN 10: 0-15-350334-3 (Grade 4 Below-Level Collection)
ISBN 13: 978-0-15-350334-4 (Grade 4 Below-Level Collection)
ISBN 10: 0-15-357533-6 (package of 5)
ISBN 13: 978-0-15-357533-4 (package of 5)

2 3 4 5 6 7 8 9 10   985   12 11 10 09 08 07

Characters

Narrator 1	Narrator 2	Worker 1	Worker 2
Carter	Lady Evelyn	Lord Carnarvon	

Setting: The tomb of King Tut

Narrator 1: In ancient Egypt, there lived a boy named Tutankhamun. In 1333 B.C., he became king.

Narrator 2: His reign was most memorable because he became king when he was only nine years old.

Narrator 1: King Tutankhamun ruled until his death at the age of eighteen.

Narrator 2: He was buried in a secret tomb surrounded by incredible riches.

Narrator 1: Thousands of years later, in the early 1900s, a distinguished archaeologist began looking for Tutankahmun's tomb. He was from England, and his name was Howard Carter.

Narrator 2: Carter examined Egyptian objects for clues that would help him discern the location of the tomb. Despite the obstacles involved, Carter dedicated himself to finding it.

Carter: I must get money so I may begin the search.

Narrator 1: Carter went to the mansion of his friend Lord Carnarvon. The mansion was in England.

Narrator 2: Lord Carnarvon's daughter, Lady Evelyn, served the two men tea.

Carter: This photo is of a cup with King Tut's name on it. We believe ancient robbers stole it from his tomb along with other items. We estimate that the robbers broke into the tomb a few thousand years ago and took away as much as they could.

Howard Carter

Lady Evelyn: Fascinating! Do you take sugar with your tea, Mr. Carter?

Carter: Yes, thank you. I believe the tomb is in the vicinity of the Valley of the Kings. I intend to find it.

Lord Carnarvon: Well, you're certainly the man to do it.

Carter: Lord Carnarvon, we could do it together, but I do need backing.

Lord Carnarvon: Something like that would take a colossal amount of money.

Lady Evelyn: It would be an adventure worth every penny. You and Mr. Carter will make history. Please, Father, say yes.

Lord Carnarvon: I never could say no to you, Evelyn.

Carter: Thank you! You won't regret this!

Narrator 1: Carter worked frantically to find the tomb.

Narrator 2: However, he wasn't having much luck. He began to run out of money.

Narrator 1: Once again, Carter went to see Lord Carnarvon and Lady Evelyn.

Narrator 2: Carter spoke of his need for more money, but Lord Carnarvon abruptly interrupted him.

Lord Carnarvon: Do you think that I'm made of money? Mr. Carter, there comes a time when a man just has to give up.

Carter: We are so close.

Lord Carnarvon: That may be just an illusion. I'm afraid my confidence is eroding.

Carter: Give me money for just one more season of digging, and I'll prove you wrong. In fact, I will make a deal with you.

Lord Carnarvon: I'm dubious, but go ahead. What is your deal?

Carter: Back me for one more season of digging. If I don't find the tomb, I'll pay back your money.

Lady Evelyn: What do you say, Father?

Lord Carnarvon: What can I say? I don't stand a chance with the two of you trying to convince me at once.

Carter: Thank you, Lord Carnarvon!

Lord Carnarvon: This is the end of it though. You have one more season to find the tomb. Understood?

Carter: Understood.

Lord Carnarvon and Howard Carter

8

Narrator 2: Back in Egypt, Carter resumed digging on November 1, 1921.

Narrator 1: At the site, Carter had his workers clearing away an ancient hut.

Worker 1: Mr. Carter, we think you should see this. It's a set of stairs.

Worker 1: They're embedded in the sand.

Carter: Dig them out!

Narrator 2: By noon the next day, the workers had completely uncovered the stairs.

Worker 2: The stairs descend to a sealed doorway.

Narrator 2: Carter went to see for himself.

Carter: Look! This is a royal seal. This could be King Tut's tomb!

Narrator 2: Carter immediately sent a telegram with this message to Lord Carnarvon.

Carter: Have made a wonderful discovery! Come right away!

Narrator 1: Lord Carnarvon and Lady Evelyn arrived at the site in Egypt as quickly as they could.

Narrator 2: The day after their arrival, Lord Carnarvon, Lady Evelyn, and a group of workers watched as Carter drilled a small hole in the door.

Lord Carnarvon: I don't think I can take the suspense. Can't you work any faster?

Carter: Sorry, I have to be careful.

Carter: There! I think that's big enough. I'll have a look inside.

Narrator 1: Carter held a candle up to the hole in the door.

Narrator 2: The air inside the tomb rushed out the hole, causing the candle to flicker.

Narrator 1: He peered inside.

Lord Carnarvon: Can you see anything?

Narrator 2: Carter was so astonished that for a moment he said nothing.

Lord Carnarvon: Carter! Carter, can you see anything?

Carter: Yes.

Lady Evelyn: What?

Carter: It's wonderful!

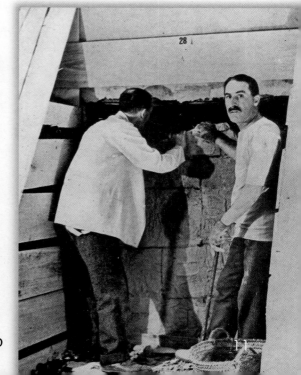

The door to
King Tut's tomb

11

Narrator 1: Soon the workers had opened the door and had brought in electric lights.

Narrator 2: Carter and the others were amazed by what they discovered.

Lady Evelyn: The air in here is actually sweet.

Carter: It's perfume.

Lady Evelyn: Do you mean I am smelling perfume that has endured for thousands of years?

Carter: Incredible, isn't it?

Lord Carnarvon: It's beyond words. Look at this throne. It's made of gold!

Lady Evelyn: These vases are beautiful.

Carter: It's all so beautiful. Everything glistens.

Inside King Tut's tomb

Narrator 1: The group scrutinized their discovery with growing astonishment.

Lady Evelyn: What is this contraption?

Carter: It is a chariot.

Lord Carnarvon: Goodness! It is made of gold!

Narrator 2: There were life-size statues of a young king with gold sandals.

Narrator 1: There were riches of all kinds.

Narrator 2: Finally, Lord Carnarvon asked the question on all their minds.

Lord Carnarvon: Carter, can we verify that this is the tomb of King Tut?

Carter: Yes.

Lady Evelyn: How can you tell?

Carter: Look at the seal over this doorway. That is the royal seal of Tutankhamun.

Lady Evelyn: Then you have truly done it. Congratulations, Mr. Carter!

Lord Carnarvon: Congratulations, indeed!

Narrator 1: It took ten years to examine and record everything found in the tomb.

Narrator 2: The findings, including the mummy of King Tutankhamun, were sent to the Egyptian Museum in Cairo, Egypt.

Narrator 1: In 1970, Tut's treasures began a tour of museums around the world. A second tour began in 2005.

Narrator 2: Thanks to Howard Carter's discovery, the whole world can see the wonderful treasures of King Tutankhamun.

Think Critically

1. In what two settings does the Readers' Theater take place?

2. How would you describe Howard Carter?

3. Why did Carter ask Lord Carnarvon for money?

4. Lord Carnarvon asked Carter if he thought that he was made of money. What did Lord Carnarvon mean by this?

5. Carter dedicated himself to a difficult goal. What goals are important to you? Why are they important?

🍁 Science

Mummy's Day The Egyptians preserved their dead as mummies for burial. Go to the library or on the Internet and research mummies. Write a brief description of what you learn.

 School-Home Connection Howard Carter and other archaeologists study objects from the past to learn about people who lived long ago. Ask a family member to help you choose an object from your home that might tell people in the future something about you and your family.

Word Count: 1,082 (1,099)